A technique long prized by restaurant chefs, sous vide cooking has gone mainstream, attracting an enthusiastic following of home cooks who appreciate its ease of use, time versatility, and consistently perfect results. Sous vide, literally "under vacuum," is the gentle cooking of food sealed in plastic and kept in constantly circulating water at a low, fixed temperature for a specified time. It yields meats that are juicy and flavorful, fish fillets that are moist and flaky, vegetables that are tender with no loss of nutrients, and fruits that soften in their own natural juices. And because the temperature of the water bath is the same as the doneness temperature, once the foods are cooked, they can be held in the water without overcooking until you're ready to serve them.

Our collection of more than 20 delicious recipes proves just how easy it is to cook sous vide. With our simple instructions on how to seal ingredients in plastic and to use an immersion circulator, this innovative technique is made fully accessible to cooks of all levels. For tender and juicy meat, try Pork Chops with Jalapeño–Agave Nectar Salsa, Greek Lamb Chops with Minted Yogurt, or Steak-Frites. For hands-off appeal, turn to Risotto with Kale Pesto, Pork Tenderloin with Cherry Chutney, or Stout-Braised Short Ribs with Herbed Mashed Potatoes. For desserts that cook then stay warm while dinner is on the table, tuck into red wine–poached pears and bourbon-infused peaches. Beautiful, full-color photographs offer mouthwatering inspiration for this contemporary cooking method.

THE
sous vide
COOKBOOK

DEVELOPED BY

WILLIAMS SONOMA

TEST KITCHEN

Photographs John Lee

weldon**owen**

Contents

Pork Chops with Jalapeño–Agave
Nectar Salsa, page 14

Honey-Dijon Salmon, page 13

UNDERSTANDING SOUS VIDE

The French term *sous vide*, literally "under vacuum," is used to describe food that is vacuum sealed in plastic for cooking in a temperature-controlled water bath. Originally used in scientific laboratories because of its precision, sous vide has since become the secret weapon of Michelin-starred chefs who appreciate the unprecedented control it affords in the kitchen. Nowadays, cooking sous vide boasts a growing and enthusiastic following among chefs and home cooks alike.

The machine that makes this precision possible is an immersion circulator, a device that both heats and then holds water at an exact temperature and continuously circulates it. It allows foods sealed in airtight bags to cook for longer times at lower temperatures than by conventional methods, resulting in perfectly cooked, intensely flavorful meats, fish, vegetables, eggs, and more. Steaks are especially tender and have a richer, meatier flavor; custards emerge flawlessly silken; and mashed potatoes, because they are not cooked in water, turn out creamier and more luscious. Sous vide also makes conventionally long-cooked dishes like short ribs an overnight proposition: put them in to cook on Tuesday evening and Wednesday's dinner will be done when it's time to set the table.

We love that sous vide frees you from standing at the stove and from tinkering with the temperature. It's a boon to busy families, too: dinner can be put on to cook just before the kids are dropped off at school and be ready to eat at the end of the day. Easy to use, an immersion circulator makes a wonderful gift for newlyweds or just-launched college grads, inspiring confidence in novice cooks and encouraging experimentation in more seasoned hands. The steady, low temperatures of sous vide cooking make it easy to put together easy, no-stress meals without fear of overcooking. And tech-savvy cooks will appreciate that some models are WiFi enabled, allowing for remote cooking: just tap the app on your phone to start cooking your meal while you're sitting at your desk or walking the dog.

TOOLS & TECHNIQUES

Cooking sous vide is remarkably simple: Put the immersion circulator in a water bath, attach the device to the side of the water container, set the temperature, seal the food in a bag, wait until the water reaches temperature, lower the bag into the water, set the time, and walk away. (To make sure the bag stays submerged and to ease its removal, attach the top of it to the side of the container using a binder clip or dedicated sous vide clip.) At the end of the cooking time, the bag can remain immersed in the water for an extended period without the food overcooking.

Cooking temperature is precisely controlled, so food never overcooks.

Food prepared sous vide retains all of its nutrients and allows for cooking with less fat.

THE IMMERSION CIRCULATOR heats and then holds the water at a precise temperature while keeping it in constant motion. It can be used in any straight-sided container, from a stockpot to a heat-resistant plastic bin to a saucepan for small bags. The container needs only to have enough room and stability to hold the immersion circulator, the bag or bags, and sufficient water to freely circulate around the bag(s).

COOKING SOUS VIDE works with both specialized vacuum bags and a dedicated vacuum sealer (pictured below) and, for some recipes, with locktop plastic freezer bags that are sealed using a water immersion and air displacement technique. Review each recipe for the method best suited to its ingredients. For a simple explanation of both methods, see page 10.

Many immersion circulators let you know when the food is ready, then keep it warm until you're ready to eat.

A vacuum sealer removes air from specialized plastic pouches, ensuring food is enclosed with both an airtight and watertight seal.

COOKING SOUS VIDE

Vacuum Seal vs. Water Immersion

A vacuum sealer delivers an airtight seal on specialized vacuum bags, making them capable of withstanding high temperatures and long cooking times. The airless environment created by vacuum sealing helps to infuse foods with the flavors of herbs, spices, garlic, and other aromatics. Some vacuum sealers can be set to remove a specific percentage of air from a bag, a feature that is particularly handy when working with delicate ingredients that can be crushed by extreme pressure. A Moist setting on some models guarantees a secure seal on juicy or marinated foods. A double seal (seal once, move the bag slightly, then seal again) is another way to ensure a good seal on wet ingredients.

Cooking sous vide is also possible without a vacuum sealer for some recipes. A water immersion and air displacement method produces an airtight seal especially suited to heartier or quickly cooking foods. To seal a bag using this method, place the ingredients in a locktop plastic freezer bag, arranging them in a single layer, and seal the bag closed except for a small opening at one corner. Holding the bag near the opening, slowly lower it into the water, leaving only the seal exposed. The barometric pressure created by the water will force out the air, creating a substantial vacuum. Seal the opening securely closed and you're ready to cook. (Be sure to use a locktop bag, not one with a sliding closure, which does not allow a complete seal.)

Cooking Times & Sous Vide

The precise temperatures of sous vide make it nearly impossible to overcook a dish. Most recipes in this book have a wide cooking window. For example, Chicken Tacos with Mexican Corn on the Cob (page 17) calls for cooking the chicken for 2–4 hours at 165°F. At any point after the first 2 hours and up to 4 hours, the chicken will remain perfectly cooked, with the internal temperature fixed at 165°F. Beyond 4 hours, the texture of the chicken will begin to deteriorate. With recipes such as steak, be sure to select the temperature for the doneness you prefer. See individual recipes for temperatures.

Completing the Process

Although steaks, chops, and burgers will be perfectly cooked when they emerge from the water bath, they will still need a swift browning for flavor and a crusty exterior. A minute or two in a very hot frying pan will give them that tasty finish.

Vacuum seal fish fillets
with aromatics such as
garlic, thyme, and lemon
to infuse extra flavor.

Honey-Dijon Salmon with Maple-Glazed Carrots

Always look for salmon that has been sustainably caught or farmed for both a healthy and a responsible choice. For a simpler side, offer broccoli rabe or chard briefly sautéed with garlic and olive oil.

Prepare an immersion circulator for use according to the manufacturer's instructions. Preheat the water to 130°F.

Season the salmon on both sides with salt and pepper, then coat on both sides with the 2 teaspoons oil. Divide the fillets, garlic, thyme sprigs, and lemon slices evenly among 4 locktop plastic freezer bags and seal the bags using the water immersion method (see page 10).

When the water reaches 130°F, lower the bags into the water bath and clip the top of each bag to the side of the water basin. Cook for 45 minutes.

Just before the salmon is ready, position an oven rack 4–6 inches from the heat source and preheat the broiler. In a small bowl, whisk together the honey and mustard, mixing well.

When the salmon is ready, remove the bags from the water bath, transfer the fillets to a plate, and pat dry. Discard the remaining contents of the bags. In a large broiler-safe frying pan over high heat, warm the remaining 1 tablespoon oil. When the oil is hot, add the salmon, skin side down, and cook until the skin is crisp, about 2 minutes. Spoon the honey-mustard mixture over the tops of the fillets and spread evenly. Transfer the pan to the broiler and broil until the honey-mustard mixture begins to bubble, about 5 minutes.

Transfer the salmon to individual plates and place the carrots alongside. Serve right away.

Water Temperature: 130°F
Time: 45 minutes
Sealing method: water immersion

SERVES 4

4 skin-on salmon fillets, 6 oz each

Kosher salt and freshly ground pepper

1 tablespoon plus 2 teaspoons extra-virgin olive oil

4 cloves garlic

8 fresh thyme sprigs

4 lemon slices

3 tablespoons honey

2 tablespoons Dijon mustard

Maple-Glazed Carrots, for serving (page 51)

Pork Chops with Jalapeño–Agave Nectar Salsa

Pork is often quite lean, and cooking it sous vide will ensure it turns out moist and tender. For the most flavorful result, look for a heritage breed, such as Berkshire or Duroc. Accompany the chops with rice pilaf and wilted greens.

Prepare an immersion circulator for use according to the manufacturer's instructions. Preheat the water to 140°F for medium-rare, 150°F for medium, or 160°F for well done.

Season the pork chops generously on both sides with salt and pepper, then sprinkle both sides evenly with the cumin. Divide the chops and onion evenly among 2 vacuum bags, arranging the chops in a single layer, and vacuum seal closed.

When the water reaches the desired temperature, lower the bags into the water bath and clip the top of each bag to the side of the water basin. Cook for 1–4 hours.

While the chops cook, make the salsa. In a bowl, stir together the jalapeño, onion, garlic, cilantro, parsley, vinegar, agave nectar, and olive oil. Season to taste with salt and pepper. Cover and refrigerate until serving.

When the pork chops are ready, remove the bags from the water bath and transfer the chops to a plate. Discard the onion. Pat the chops dry and let rest for 10 minutes.

Preheat a stovetop grill pan over high heat until hot. Brush with the grapeseed oil. Add the chops and sear, turning once, until charred and golden, about 2 minutes per side.

Transfer the chops to individual plates and finish with the sea salt. Serve right away, with the salsa alongside.

Water Temperature: 140°F for medium-rare, 150°F for medium, or 160°F for well done
Time: 1–4 hours
Sealing Method: vacuum seal

SERVES 4

4 bone-in loin pork chops, each 1½ inches thick (about 2½ lb total)

Kosher salt and freshly ground pepper

1 teaspoon ground cumin

½ red onion, thinly sliced

FOR THE SALSA

1 jalapeño chile, seeded and minced

½ red onion, finely diced

2 cloves garlic, minced

1 cup fresh cilantro leaves, roughly chopped

½ cup fresh flat-leaf parsley leaves, roughly chopped

¼ cup sherry vinegar

1½ tablespoons agave nectar

2 tablespoons extra-virgin olive oil

Kosher salt and freshly ground pepper

2 tablespoons grapeseed oil

Flaky sea salt, for finishing

Serve the ears of corn alongside, or cut the kernels from the cobs and add them to the tacos with the cheese and sour cream topping.

Chicken Tacos with Mexican Corn on the Cob

You can also dress up these tacos with a favorite salsa, thinly sliced radishes, and/or pickled carrots and jalapeños. Offer pinto beans along with the corn, and finish the meal with *dulce de leche* ice cream.

Prepare an immersion circulator for use according to the manufacturer's instructions. Preheat the water to 165°F.

In a large bowl, whisk together the chipotle chiles, adobo sauce, garlic, tomato purée, lime juice, honey, cumin, coriander, chile powder, 1½ teaspoons salt, and ½ teaspoon pepper. Add the chicken thighs and toss to coat evenly with the sauce. Transfer the thighs and sauce to a large locktop plastic freezer bag, arranging the thighs in a single layer, and seal using the water immersion method (see page 10).

When the water reaches 165°F, lower the bag into the water bath and clip the top of the bag to the side of the water basin. Cook for 2–4 hours. (Beyond 4 hours, the texture of the chicken begins to deteriorate.)

When the chicken is ready, remove the bag from the water bath and transfer the thighs to a cutting board to rest for 15 minutes. Pour the cooking liquid into a measuring cup.

Remove and discard the skin and bones from the chicken. Cut chicken into bite-size pieces and transfer to a bowl. Add about 1 cup of the reserved cooking liquid and toss to coat well. Season to taste with salt, pepper, and lime juice.

Spoon the chicken and sauce onto warmed tortillas and top with sour cream and cilantro. Serve right away, accompanied with the corn.

Water Temperature: 165°F
Time: 2–4 hours
Sealing Method: water immersion

SERVES 4

2 chipotle chiles in adobo sauce, minced, plus 1 tablespoon sauce

2 cloves garlic, minced

¼ cup tomato purée

1 tablespoon fresh lime juice, plus more for seasoning

1 teaspoon honey

1 teaspoon ground cumin

1 teaspoon ground coriander

1 teaspoon ancho chile powder

Kosher salt and freshly ground pepper

2 lb bone-in, skin-on chicken thighs

8 corn tortillas, warmed

Sour cream and fresh cilantro, for serving

Mexican Corn on the Cob, for serving (page 52)

Greek Lamb Chops with Minted Yogurt

Basting the seared lamb with sizzling butter just before serving gives the meat a more uniform crust and richer flavor. Cucumber salad is an ideal accompaniment.

To make the lamb, prepare an immersion circulator for use according to the manufacturer's instructions. Preheat the water to 136°F for medium-rare or 140°F for medium.

Season the lamb chops with salt and pepper. Divide the chops, oregano, lemon wedges, and garlic between 2 vacuum bags, arranging the chops in a single layer, and vacuum seal closed.

When the water reaches the desired temperature, lower the bags into the water bath. Cook for 1–3 hours.

Meanwhile, make the yogurt: In a small bowl, combine all the ingredients and mix well. Cover and refrigerate for at least 1 hour or up to 1 day. Make the salad and set aside.

When the lamb is ready, remove the bag from the water bath. Transfer the chops to a plate. Reserve the herbs, lemon, and garlic. Pat the chops dry and season with salt and pepper.

Heat a large frying pan over high heat until very hot. Melt 2 tablespoons of the butter in the pan, add half of the lamb chops, and sear, turning once, until evenly browned, about 1 minute per side. Transfer to a platter. Repeat with the remaining 2 tablespoons butter and the remaining lamb chops. Add the reserved oregano, lemon wedges, and garlic to the pan and cook, stirring as needed, until charred, about 3 minutes. Return all the chops to the pan and, using a spoon, baste with the butter for about 30 seconds.

Serve the chops with the yogurt, salad, and charred oregano, garlic, and lemon wedges alongside.

Water Temperature: 136°F for medium-rare, 140°F for medium, or 145°F for well done
Time: 1–3 hours
Sealing Method: vacuum seal

SERVES 4

FOR THE LAMB

8 lamb rib chops, about 1 inch thick, trimmed of fat

Kosher salt and freshly ground pepper

6 fresh oregano sprigs

2 lemon wedges

6 cloves garlic, smashed

4 tablespoons unsalted butter

FOR THE YOGURT

1 cup plain Greek yogurt

½ cup very finely chopped fresh mint

1 tablespoon fresh lemon juice

½ teaspoon ground cumin

½ teaspoon granulated garlic

Pinch of cayenne pepper

Kosher salt and freshly ground black pepper

Tomato-Cucumber Salad, for serving (page 52)

Serve the minted yogurt alongside for dipping, as here, or divide it evenly among individual plates and arrange the lamb chops on top.

Cheeseburgers with Gruyère & Onions

You can customize these cheeseburgers, using your favorite bread in place of the brioche buns and your preferred cheese in place of the Gruyère.

Prepare an immersion circulator for use according to the manufacturer's instructions. Preheat the water to 125°F for medium-rare, 135°F for medium, or 140°F for medium-well.

Divide the beef into 5 equal portions. Form each portion into a patty about 3½ inches in diameter and 1 inch thick. Season generously on both sides with salt and pepper. Place each patty in a small locktop plastic freezer bag and seal using the water immersion method (see page 10). When the water reaches the desired temperature, lower the bags into the water bath and clip the top of each bag to the side of the water basin. Cook for 40 minutes–2 hours.

While the patties cook, make the onions. In a large sauté pan over medium heat, combine the onions, oil, and water and cook, stirring occasionally, until the onions are very tender and golden, about 20 minutes. Add both vinegars and cook until no liquid remains, about 3 minutes more. Season with salt and pepper. Remove from the heat.

When the patties are ready, remove the bags from the water bath and transfer the patties to a plate. Pat the patties dry and let rest for 10 minutes.

In a frying pan over high heat, warm the oil. Add the patties and sear on the first side until charred, about 2 minutes. Flip the patties, add the cheese, and cook until charred on the second side and the cheese is melted, about 3 minutes.

Divide the onions equally among the bun bottoms, then top each with a burger. Close with the bun tops and serve.

Water Temperature: 125°F for medium-rare, 135°F for medium, or 140°F for medium-well

Time: 40 minutes–2 hours

Sealing Method: water immersion

SERVES 5

2 lb ground beef

Kosher salt and freshly ground pepper

FOR THE ONIONS

2 yellow onions, thinly sliced

2 tablespoons extra-virgin olive oil

1 tablespoon water

2 tablespoons balsamic vinegar

2 tablespoons red wine vinegar

Kosher salt and freshly ground pepper

2 tablespoons extra-virgin olive oil

5 oz Gruyère cheese, cut into 5 equal slices

5 brioche hamburger buns, split

Chipotle–Butternut Squash Soup

Cooked conventionally, this subtly spiced squash soup would call for stirring and adjusting the heat every now and again. But using sous vide makes it a hands-off recipe ideal for a cool-weather supper.

Prepare an immersion circulator for use according to the manufacturer's instructions. Preheat the water to 185°F.

Place the squash, onion, garlic, 2 teaspoons salt, and the chile (use the smaller amount for less spice) in a large vacuum bag, arranging the squash cubes in a single layer, and vacuum seal closed.

When the water reaches 185°F, lower the bag into the water bath and clip the top of the bag to the side of the water basin. Cook for 1–2 hours.

When the squash is ready, remove the bag from the water bath and transfer the contents to a blender. Add the broth and process on high speed until smooth, about 1 minute. Transfer the soup to a saucepan and place over medium heat. Stir in the vinegar, crème fraîche, and maple syrup, and season to taste with salt and pepper. If desired, add 1–2 teaspoons adobo sauce for extra heat. Warm, stirring occasionally, until piping hot.

Ladle the soup into individual bowls and top each bowl with a dollop of crème fraîche, a pinch each of chili powder and sea salt, and a sprinkle of pecans. Serve right away.

Temperature: 185°F
Time: 1–2 hours
Sealing Method: vacuum seal

SERVES 4

1 butternut squash, about 3 lb, halved, seeded, peeled, and cut into 1-inch cubes (about 4 cups)

1 yellow onion, chopped

1 clove garlic, peeled

Kosher salt and freshly ground pepper

½–1 chipotle chile in adobo sauce, plus 1–2 teaspoons sauce (optional)

2 cups vegetable or chicken broth

1 teaspoon sherry vinegar

¼ cup crème fraîche, plus more for topping

1 tablespoon maple syrup

Chili powder, for finishing

Flaky sea salt, for finishing

⅓ cup toasted chopped pecans

A garnish of fresh
watercress leaves adds
color to the bowls just
before serving.

Garlic-Potato Soup with Poached Egg

You can alter the seasoning of this wintry soup by using thyme in place of the rosemary, or equal amounts of rosemary and thyme. If watercress is not in the market, flat-leaf parsley is a good substitute.

Prepare an immersion circulator for use according to the manufacturer's instructions. Preheat the water to 185°F.

In a sauté pan over medium heat, warm the oil. Add the onion and cook, stirring occasionally, until tender, about 4 minutes. Add the garlic and cook until fragrant, about 1 minute more. Remove from the heat and let cool.

Place the potatoes, butter, rosemary, 1 tablespoon salt, 1 teaspoon pepper, and the cooled onion mixture in a large locktop plastic freezer bag and seal using the water immersion method (see page 10).

When the water reaches 185°F, lower the bag into the water bath and clip the top of the bag to the side of the water basin. Cook until the potatoes are very tender, 1½–3 hours.

When the potatoes are ready, remove the bag from the water bath. In batches, transfer the contents of the bag to a blender. Add the cream and the 2 cups water and process, starting on low speed and gradually increasing to high speed, until smooth, about 4 minutes. Add more water if needed to achieve the desired consistency. Transfer to a large saucepan, stir in the lemon juice and crème fraîche, and heat gently until piping hot. Season to taste with salt and pepper.

Ladle the soup into individual bowls. Top each bowl with an egg, then garnish with the watercress and finish with a grinding of pepper. Serve right away.

Water Temperature: 185°F
Time: 1½–3 hours
Sealing Method: water immersion

SERVES 6

2 tablespoons extra-virgin olive oil

1 yellow onion, diced

4 cloves garlic, thinly sliced

1¾ lb Yukon gold potatoes, unpeeled and thinly sliced

4 tablespoons unsalted butter

3 fresh rosemary sprigs

Kosher salt and freshly ground pepper

1 cup heavy cream

2 cups water, plus more as needed

Juice of 1 lemon

½ cup crème fraîche

6 poached eggs (page 52)

Watercress leaves, for garnish

Steak-Frites with Rosemary Garlic Butter

A French bistro classic, *steak-frites* needs only a green salad and a good Cabernet or Merlot to complete the meal. Originally a no-frills worker's dish, the steak is now a universal favorite and is often treated to last-minute spoonful of béarnaise sauce. Here, a simple herb-garlic butter crowns well-seasoned meat.

Prepare an immersion circulator for use according to the manufacturer's instructions. Preheat the water to 129°F for medium-rare or 134°F for medium.

Season the steaks generously on both sides with salt and pepper. Place each steak in a vacuum bag, add 1 of the rosemary sprigs and 2 of the garlic cloves to each bag, and vacuum seal closed.

When the water reaches the desired temperature, lower the bags into the water bath and clip the top of each bag to the side of the water basin. Cook the steaks for 1–4 hours. When the steaks are ready, remove the bags from the water bath, transfer the steaks to a plate, and discard the rosemary and garlic. Pat the steaks dry. Season with salt and pepper.

Heat a large frying pan over high heat until very hot. Add the oil, and when the oil is hot, add the steaks and sear, turning once, until a charred crust forms on both sides, about 2 minutes per side. Add the butter and the remaining 4 garlic cloves and 2 rosemary sprigs to the pan. When the butter melts, using a spoon, baste the steaks with the butter for about 1 minute, placing the garlic and rosemary on the steaks if they begin to burn.

Serve the steaks right away, accompanied with the frites.

Water Temperature: 129°F for medium-rare steaks, or 134°F for medium

Time: 1–4 hours

Sealing Method: vacuum seal

SERVES 2–4

2 boneless rib-eye or strip steaks, about ¾ lb each

Kosher salt and freshly ground pepper

4 fresh rosemary sprigs

8 cloves garlic, smashed

2 tablespoons canola oil

4 tablespoons unsalted butter

Frites, for serving (page 50)

A quick sear in a hot pan is all that's required to cook steaks prepped via sous vide to juicy perfection.

Although some liquid may remain after cooking, the rice will soon absorb it. For the best results, cook the risotto within an hour of filling and sealing the bags.

Risotto with Kale Pesto, Mozzarella & Cherry Tomatoes

Sous vide takes much of the work out of cooking risotto—no standing at the stove stirring constantly—leaving you free to ready the rest of the meal. If you prefer a more traditional pesto, omit the kale and use 2 cups basil leaves.

Prepare an immersion circulator for use according to the manufacturer's instructions. Preheat the water to 185°F.

Place the rice, broth, salt, and pepper in a large locktop plastic freezer bag and seal using the water immersion method (see page 10).

When the water reaches 185°F, lower the bag into the water bath and clip the top of the bag to the side of the water basin. Cook for 1 hour. Most of the liquid will be absorbed.

While the rice cooks, make the pesto. In a blender or small food processor, combine the kale, basil, pine nuts, Parmesan, oil, and lemon juice and process until almost smooth. Season to taste with salt and pepper.

When the rice is ready, remove the bag from the water bath and empty the contents into a bowl. Stir in the pesto and season to taste with salt and pepper.

Transfer the risotto to individual shallow bowls and garnish with the tomatoes, mozzarella, and basil. Serve right away.

Water Temperature: 185°F
Time: 1 hour
Sealing Method: water immersion

SERVES 4

1 cup Arborio rice

3 cups chicken or vegetable broth

1 teaspoon kosher salt

½ teaspoon freshly ground pepper

FOR THE PESTO

1 cup kale leaves, roughly chopped

1 cup fresh basil leaves

¼ cup pine nuts, toasted

¼ cup grated Parmesan cheese

¾ cup extra-virgin olive oil

Juice of 1 lemon

Kosher salt and freshly ground pepper

FOR GARNISH

1 cup cherry tomatoes, halved

½ lb fresh mozzarella cheese, sliced

Fresh basil leaves

Ginger Shrimp with Baby Bok Choy

On the stovetop, shrimp can quickly go from pearly pink and tender to tough and rubbery if cooked too long. Here, steady sous vide heat guarantees even cooking.

To make the shrimp, prepare an immersion circulator for use according to the manufacturer's instructions. Preheat the water to 140°F.

In a bowl, toss the shrimp with the baking soda and salt. In a small saucepan over medium heat, combine the coconut oil, garlic, and ginger and cook, stirring occasionally, until fragrant, about 2 minutes. Remove from the heat, stir in the green onion and vinegar, and let cool for 5 minutes.

In a gallon-size locktop plastic freezer bag, combine the cooled coconut oil mixture and the shrimp in a single layer, and seal using the water immersion method (see page 10).

When the water reaches 140°F, lower the bag into the water bath and clip the top of the bag to the side of the water basin. Cook for 25 minutes.

While the shrimp cook, make the vegetables. In a large frying pan over medium-high heat, warm the vegetable oil. Add the bok choy, garlic, and red pepper flakes and cook, stirring often, until the bok choy begins to wilt, about 2 minutes. Add the edamame, soy sauce, and water and continue to cook, stirring often, until the bok choy is tender, about 2 minutes. Stir in the fish sauce and sesame oil, then taste and adjust with more fish sauce and sesame oil if needed. Keep warm.

When the shrimp are ready, remove the bag from the water bath. Spoon the bok choy mixture onto a platter and top with the shrimp. Garnish with the green onion and sesame seeds and serve right away.

Water Temperature: 140°F
Time: 25 minutes
Sealing Method: water immersion

SERVES 4

FOR THE SHRIMP

1 lb shrimp, peeled and deveined, tails intact

½ teaspoon baking soda

½ teaspoon kosher salt

2 tablespoons coconut oil

3 cloves garlic, smashed

1-inch piece fresh ginger, peeled and thinly sliced

2 tablespoons thinly sliced green onion

2 teaspoons rice vinegar

FOR THE VEGETABLES

1 tablespoon canola oil

1½ lb baby bok choy, cut into 1-inch pieces

1 clove garlic, minced

½ teaspoon red pepper flakes

1 cup frozen shelled edamame, thawed

1 tablespoon soy sauce

1 tablespoon water

1 teaspoon fish sauce

¼ teaspoon Asian sesame oil

2 tablespoons thinly sliced green onion

1 tablespoon sesame seeds, toasted

Lobster Roll Sliders

The tender, moist butter-poached lobster meat that emerges from a water bath is one of the best reasons to cook sous vide. Serve with chips and pickles on the side.

Prepare an immersion circulator for use according to the manufacturer's instructions. Preheat the water to 130°F.

Have ready an ice-water bath. Bring a large pot three-fourths full of salted water to a boil over high heat. Add the lobster tails and boil until the shells begin to turn red, about 3 minutes. Transfer the tails to the ice bath. Crack the tails and remove the meat from each one in a single piece.

Divide the lobster meat evenly among 2 small locktop plastic freezer bags. Add 5 chives, 1 lemon quarter, 2 tablespoons of the butter, and a pinch of salt to each bag. Arrange the lobster meat in a single layer and seal the bags using the water immersion method (see page 10).

When the water reaches 130°F, lower the bags into the water bath and clip to the basin side. Cook for 30–60 minutes.

When the lobster is ready, remove the bags from the water bath and let rest for 5 minutes. Reserve 1 tablespoon of the cooking liquid from the bags. Cut the lobster into 1-inch pieces, transfer to a bowl, and refrigerate for 15 minutes.

In a bowl, mix the mayonnaise, green onion, celery, and reserved cooking liquid. Add the chilled lobster and mix gently. Season to taste with salt and pepper.

Spread the remaining 4 tablespoons butter over the cut sides of the buns. Heat a frying pan over medium-high heat. Toast the buns, buttered sides down, until golden, about 2 minutes.

Top the bun bottoms with the lobster, dividing evenly, then close with the bun tops. Serve with the remaining lemons.

Water Temperature: 130°F
Time: 30–60 minutes
Sealing Method: water immersion

SERVES 4–6

2 lb lobster tails

10 fresh chives

1 lemon, quartered

8 tablespoons unsalted butter

Kosher salt and freshly ground pepper

⅓ cup mayonnaise

2 tablespoons minced green onion

2 tablespoons minced celery

6 brioche slider buns

Black Cod with Tarragon Cream Sauce

Infused with the bright flavors of the aromatics with which it is vacuum packed, velvety textured black cod is particulary delicious when cooked sous vide.

To make the cod, prepare an immersion circulator for use according to the manufacturer's instructions. Preheat the water to 130°F.

Season the cod with salt and pepper. Divide the fillets, butter, tarragon sprigs, lemon slices, and shallot quarters evenly among 4 small locktop plastic freezer bags and seal the bags using the water immersion method (see page 10).

When the water reaches 130°F, lower the bags into the water bath and clip to the basin side. Cook for 30 minutes.

While the cod cooks, roast the asparagus and make the sauce. Preheat the oven to 425°F. Place the asparagus on a baking sheet, drizzle with the oil, and toss to coat evenly. Season with salt and pepper and spread in a single layer. Roast until crisp-tender, 10–12 minutes.

In a small saucepan over medium-low heat, warm the oil and butter. Add the shallot and cook, stirring often, until softened, about 3 minutes. Stir in the flour and cook, stirring, for 1 minute. Whisk in the wine and tarragon and cook, whisking often, until thickened, about 3 minutes. Whisk in the cream and salt and heat until hot, about 2 minutes. Keep warm.

When the cod is ready, remove the bags from the water bath, transfer the fillets to a plate, and pat dry. In a large frying pan over high heat, warm the oil. Add the fish, skin side down, and cook until the skin is crisp, about 2 minutes.

Place the cod and asparagus on individual plates. Spoon the cream sauce over the cod, garnish with tarragon, and serve.

Water Temperature: 130°F
Time: 30 minutes
Sealing Method: water immersion

SERVES 4

FOR THE COD

4 skin-on black cod fillets, 4 oz each

Kosher salt and freshly ground pepper

2 tablespoons unsalted butter

4 fresh tarragon sprigs

4 lemon slices

1 shallot, quartered

1 tablespoon extra-virgin olive oil

FOR THE ASPARAGUS

1 lb asparagus, ends trimmed

1 tablespoon extra-virgin olive oil

Kosher salt and freshly ground pepper

FOR THE SAUCE

1 tablespoon olive oil

1 tablespoon unsalted butter

1 shallot, minced

1 tablespoon all-purpose flour

1 cup dry white wine

2 teaspoons minced fresh tarragon

½ cup heavy cream

½ teaspoon kosher salt

Minced fresh tarragon, for garnish

Any firm-textured fish fillet can stand in for the cod. Try halibut, sea bass, or snapper.

For a simpler, less rich dish, subsitute steamed white basmati or jasmine rice for the polenta.

Brown Butter Scallops with Polenta

Look for environmentally friendly diver scallops (harvested by hand from the ocean floor) for the best flavor. A fresh herb salad is a lovely accompaniment.

To make the scallops, prepare an immersion circulator for use according to the manufacturer's instructions. Preheat the water to 140°F.

Season the scallops with salt and pepper. Divide the scallops, thyme, and tarragon evenly between 2 small vacuum bags and add 2 tablespoons butter to each bag. Arrange the scallops in a single layer and vacuum seal closed.

When the water reaches 140°F, lower the bags into the water bath. Cook the scallops until tender, 35–45 minutes.

Meanwhile, in a large bowl, combine the cilantro, parsley, dill, basil, and mâche and toss to mix. Just before serving, season generously with salt and pepper, drizzle with the oil and vinegar, and toss gently to coat. Cook the polenta; set aside.

When the scallops are ready, remove the bags from the water bath and transfer the scallops to a plate. Discard the herb sprigs. Pat the scallops dry and season with salt and pepper.

Heat a large sauté pan over high heat until very hot and add 1 tablespoon of the remaining butter. Working in batches, add the scallops and sear, turning once, to form a golden crust, about 1 minute per side. Transfer the scallops to a plate. Reduce the heat to medium-low and add the remaining 4 tablespoons butter to the pan. Cook until browned and fragrant, about 5 minutes; do not burn. Return the scallops to the pan and baste with the browned butter for 30 seconds.

Divide the polenta among individual plates. Spoon the scallops over the polenta. Serve with the salad alongside.

Water Temperature: 140°F
Time: 35–45 minutes
Sealing Method: vacuum seal

SERVES 4

FOR THE SCALLOPS

1 lb sea scallops, side muscle removed (about 16 scallops)

Kosher salt and freshly ground pepper

2 fresh tarragon sprigs

2 fresh thyme sprigs

4 tablespoons unsalted butter, cut into 1-tablespoon pieces, plus 5 tablespoons

FOR THE SALAD

1 cup lightly packed fresh cilantro leaves

1 cup lightly packed fresh flat-leaf parsley leaves

1 cup lightly packed fresh dill leaves

1 cup fresh basil leaves, cut into chiffonade

1½ cups mâche or baby arugula

Kosher salt and freshly ground pepper

2 tablespoons extra-virgin olive oil

2 teaspoons white wine vinegar

Parmesan Polenta (page 50)

Salt & Vinegar Chicken Wings

Cooking chicken wings with the low, controlled heat of sous vide helps to break down their connective tissue, creating tender meat that crisps beautifully when fried.

Prepare an immersion circulator for use according to the manufacturer's instructions. Preheat the water to 165°F.

In a small bowl, whisk together the vinegars, olive oil, sugar, salt, garlic powder, and pepper. Reserve ¼ cup of the mixture. In a gallon-size locktop plastic freezer bag, combine the chicken wings with the remaining vinegar mixture, arranging the wings in a single layer, and seal using the water immersion method (see page 10).

When the water reaches 165°F, lower the bag into the water bath and clip the top of the bag to the side of the water basin. Cook for 4 hours. When the chicken is ready, remove the bag from the water bath and transfer the wings to a paper towel–lined baking sheet, arranging them in a single layer. Let cool for 30 minutes.

Meanwhile, make the aioli. In a small bowl, stir together the mayonnaise, harissa sauce, lime juice, and garlic, mixing well. Season to taste with salt and pepper and with additional lime juice if needed. Cover and refrigerate until serving.

Pour vegetable oil to a depth of 2 inches in a heavy saucepan and heat to 375°F on a deep-frying thermometer. Line a baking sheet with paper towels. Working in batches, fry the wings until deep golden brown, about 3 minutes. Using tongs, transfer the wings to the prepared baking sheet to drain.

When all the wings are fried, transfer them to a large bowl, add the reserved vinegar mixture and sea salt, and toss to mix well. Serve immediately with the aioli.

Water Temperature: 165°F
Time: 3–4 hours
Sealing method: water immersion

SERVES 4

½ cup distilled white vinegar

¼ cup cider vinegar

2 tablespoons extra-virgin olive oil

2 teaspoons sugar

2 teaspoons kosher salt

1 teaspoon garlic powder

½ teaspoon freshly ground pepper

2 lb chicken wings

Vegetable oil, for frying

Generous pinch of flaky sea salt

FOR THE HARISSA AIOLI

½ cup mayonnaise

2 tablespoons harissa sauce

1 teaspoon fresh lime juice, plus more if needed

1 clove garlic, grated

Kosher salt and freshly ground pepper

A last-minute sprinkling of flaky sea salt brings a hit of unexpected flavor to tender, richly browned wings.

Cherry chutney adds a sweet-sour accent to mildly-flavored pork tenderloin. If you are short on time, serve the pork with a purchased plum or peach chutney instead.

Pork Tenderloin with Cherry Chutney

Chinese five-spice offers inimitable flavor to pork tenderloin, the leanest, mildest cut from the pig. Spiced cherry chutney offers a fruity complement to the meat.

Prepare an immersion circulator for use according to the manufacturer's instructions. Preheat the water to 130°F for medium-rare, 145° for medium, or 160°F for well done.

Season the pork generously with salt and pepper, then rub on all sides with the five-spice powder. Place the pork in a vacuum bag and vacuum seal closed.

When the water reaches the desired temperature, lower the bag into the water bath and clip the top of the bag to the side of the water basin. Cook for 1–4 hours.

Meanwhile, make the chutney:. In a sauté pan over medium heat, warm the oil. Add the shallot and cook, stirring, until tender, about 2 minutes. Stir in the cherries. Add both vinegars and cook, stirring often, until the cherries are tender, about 5 minutes. Stir in the mustard seeds, nutmeg, cloves, and brown sugar. Cook until the liquid is reduced to a syrupy glaze, about 10 minutes. Remove from the heat. Season to taste with salt, pepper, and more sugar if needed. Let cool.

When the pork is ready, remove the bag from the water bath, transfer the pork to a plate, and pat dry. In a large frying pan over medium-high heat, warm the oil. Add the tenderloin and sear on all sides until golden brown, about 2 minutes per side. Transfer to a cutting board, tent with aluminum foil, and let rest for 10 minutes.

Slice the pork against the grain. Divide the mash among individual plates and top with the pork. Top with the chutney and celery leaves, finish with sea salt, and serve.

Water Temperature: 130°F for medium-rare, 145° for medium, or 160°F for well done
Time: 1–4 hours
Sealing Method: vacuum seal

SERVES 4

1 pork tenderloin, 1¾ lb

Kosher salt and freshly ground pepper

1 teaspoon five-spice powder

FOR THE CHUTNEY

1 tablespoon extra-virgin olive oil

1 shallot, minced

1 cup dried cherries, soaked in water for 30 minutes then drained

⅓ cup cider vinegar

⅓ cup red wine vinegar

2 tablespoons yellow mustard seeds

¼ teaspoon ground nutmeg

Pinch of ground cloves

3 tablespoons firmly packed golden brown sugar, plus more to taste (optional)

Kosher salt and freshly ground pepper

2 tablespoons extra-virgin olive oil

Potato–Celery Root Mash, for serving (page 51)

Fresh celery leaves, for garnish

Flaky sea salt, for finishing

Chicken Thighs with Lemon, Honey & Green Olives

Coating the chicken thighs with a mixture of butter and honey before they go into the water bath gives them a particularly juicy, succulent texture, while a quick sear just before serving provides a flavorful caramelized finish.

Prepare an immersion circulator for use according to the manufacturer's instructions. Preheat the water to 150°F.

In a small bowl, combine the butter, honey, and lemon zest and mix well. Season the chicken thighs generously with kosher salt and pepper and rub all over with the butter mixture. Place the thighs and garlic in a vacuum bag, arranging the thighs in a single layer, and vacuum seal closed.

When the water reaches 150°F, lower the bags into the water bath and clip the top of the bags to the side of the water basin. Cook for 1–1½ hours.

When the chicken is ready, remove the bags from the water bath, transfer the thighs to a large plate, and pat them dry.

In a large sauté pan over medium-high heat, warm the oil. Add the chicken, skin side down, and sear until golden brown, about 3 minutes. Transfer to individual plates and sprinkle with the olives. Finish with a sprinkle of sea salt and garnish with fennel fronds. Serve right away.

2 tablespoons unsalted butter, at room temperature

1 tablespoon honey

Grated zest of 1 lemon

2 lb boneless, skin-on chicken thighs

Kosher salt and freshly ground black pepper

2 cloves garlic, smashed

2 tablespoons extra-virgin olive oil

½ cup chopped green olives

Flaky sea salt, for finishing

Fennel fronds or fresh herbs of choice, for garnish

Water Temperature: 150°F
Time: 1–1½ hours
Sealing method: vacuum seal

SERVES 4–6

Stout-Braised Short Ribs with Herbed Mashed Potatoes

Short ribs are the perfect candidate for sous vide cooking. The tough, richly marbled cut turns out tender and moist after a 24-hour stint in the low, steady heat of a water bath. The braising medium of dark, malty stout complements the hearty beef.

Prepare an immersion circulator for use according to the manufacturer's instructions. Preheat the water to 170°F.

Season the ribs generously all over with salt and pepper. In a large frying pan over medium-high heat, warm the oil. Working in batches, brown the ribs on all sides, about 12 minutes total per batch. Transfer the ribs to a plate.

Add the onion, carrot, celery, and garlic to the same pan over medium-high heat and cook, stirring occasionally, until softened, about 5 minutes. Add the stout, demi-glace, tomato paste, and pepper flakes, stir well, and bring to a boil. Reduce the heat to a simmer and cook until the liquid is reduced by half, about 5 minutes. Season to taste with salt, pepper, and a squeeze of juice from the lemon half, then remove from the heat and let cool to room temperature, about 1 hour.

Divide the ribs evenly between 2 vacuum bags and add half of the liquid to each bag. Arrange the ribs in a single layer and double vacuum seal both ends of each bag (see page 10).

Lower the bags into the water bath and clip the top of the bags to the side of the water basin. Cover with the basin lid or plastic wrap and cook for 24 hours.

When the ribs are ready, remove the bags from the water bath and transfer the ribs to a platter. Spoon the liquid from the bag over the ribs and serve with the potatoes.

Water Temperature: 170°F
Time: 24 hours
Sealing Method: vacuum seal

SERVES 4

4 lb bone-in beef short ribs

Kosher salt and freshly ground pepper

1 tablespoon extra-virgin olive oil

1 small yellow onion, finely diced

1 large carrot finely diced

1 celery stalk, finely diced

3 cloves garlic, minced

1 cup dry stout, such as Guinness

2 tablespoons beef or veal demi-glace

1 tablespoon tomato paste

½ teaspoon red pepper flakes

½ lemon

4 fresh flat-leaf parsley sprigs

4 fresh thyme sprigs

Herbed Mashed Potatoes, for serving (page 51)

Turkey with Sage & Garlic

Here is the ideal recipe for Thanksgiving: It frees up the oven for other dishes, and cooking the turkey sous vide ensures moist and tender meat.

To make the brine, in a small saucepan, combine 2 cups of the water, the kosher salt, brown sugar, peppercorns, allspice, and bay leaf. Bring to a boil over high heat and stir until the salt dissolves, about 3 minutes. Transfer to a large pot, add the remaining 10 cups water, and stir well. Let cool. Immerse the turkey breast in the brine. Cover and refrigerate overnight.

Prepare an immersion circulator for use according to the manufacturer's instructions. Preheat the water to 156°F.

To make the rub, in a small bowl, stir together the butter, brown sugar, minced garlic, garlic powder, sage, salt, and pepper, mixing well. Remove the turkey from the brine and pat dry. Rub all over with the butter mixture, then place in a large vacuum bag and vacuum seal closed.

When the water reaches 156°F, lower the bag into the water bath and clip to the basin side. Cook the turkey for 2–4 hours.

Just before the turkey is ready, in a large sauté pan over medium heat, warm 4 tablespoons of the oil. Add the sage leaves and cook until crisp, 30–60 seconds. Transfer the leaves to a paper towel–lined plate. Set the pan aside.

When the turkey is ready, remove the bag from the water bath, transfer the turkey to a plate, and pat dry. Add the remaining 2 tablespoons oil to the sauté pan and warm over medium heat.Add the turkey, skin side down, and sear until the skin is golden brown and crisp, about 4 minutes. Transfer to a cutting board, tent with aluminum foil, and let rest for 10 minutes.

Carve the turkey. Serve topped with sea salt and fried sage.

Water Temperature: 156°F
Time: 2–4 hours
Sealing Method: vacuum seal

SERVES 6–12

FOR THE BRINE

12 cups water

¼ cup kosher salt

2 tablespoons firmly packed light brown sugar

1 tablespoon peppercorns

1 teaspoon allspice berries

1 bay leaf

1 bone-in, skin-on turkey breast, 3–5 lb

FOR THE RUB

3 tablespoons unsalted butter, at room temperature

2 tablespoons firmly packed light brown sugar

2 cloves garlic, minced

1 teaspoon garlic powder

2 tablespoons finely chopped fresh sage

½ teaspoon kosher salt

½ teaspoon freshly ground pepper

6 tablespoons extra-virgin olive oil

12 fresh sage leaves

Flaky sea salt, for finishing

To prepare the peaches in advance, place them in a vaccum bag, seal closed, and refrigerate for up to 12 hours before cooking.

Bourbon-Infused Peaches with Streusel

These summery poached peaches are also delicious made with dark rum in place of the bourbon and hazelnuts standing in for the almonds.

To make the peaches, prepare an immersion circulator for use according to the manufacturer's instructions. Preheat the water 180°F.

In a small saucepan over medium-high heat, combine the water and sugar and bring to a boil, stirring to dissolve the sugar. Cook, stirring occasionally, until slightly thickened, about 5 minutes. Add the bourbon and vanilla bean seeds and cook for 1 minute more, then remove from the heat.

Place the peach halves and bourbon syrup in a vacuum bag, arranging the peaches in a single layer, and vacuum seal closed, taking care not to crush the delicate fruit.

When the water reaches 180°F, lower the bag into the water bath and clip the top of the bag to the side of the water basin. Cook the peaches for 30–45 minutes, depending on ripeness.

While the peaches are cooking, make the topping. In a bowl, whisk together the flour, brown sugar, salt, and cinnamon. In a nonstick 10-inch frying pan over medium heat, melt the butter. Remove from the heat and stir in the flour mixture until small clumps form and all the butter is absorbed. Return the pan to low heat, add the almonds, and cook, stirring often, until the streusel is light golden brown, about 5 minutes. Transfer to a plate to cool.

When the peaches are ready, remove the bag from the water bath. Place 2 peach halves in each individual bowl. Serve right away, topped with the syrup from the bag, the streusel topping, and the ice cream.

Water Temperature: 180°F
Time: 30–45 minutes
Sealing Method: vacuum seal

SERVES 4

FOR THE PEACHES

1 cup water

1 cup sugar

¾ cup bourbon

½ vanilla bean, split lengthwise and seeds removed

4 peaches, halved and pitted

FOR THE TOPPING

1 cup all-purpose flour

½ cup firmly packed light brown sugar

1 teaspoon kosher salt

1 teaspoon ground cinnamon

½ cup unsalted butter

½ cup slivered blanched almonds

Vanilla ice cream, for serving

Classic Crème Brûlée

Making a custard on the stovetop can be tricky. Too hot, and the custard will curdle. The steady heat of a sous vide bath ensures that the custard be rich, smooth, and creamy—the perfect base for a brittle, crackly topping of burned sugar.

Prepare an immersion circulator for use according to the manufacturer's instructions. Preheat the water to 176°F.

In a saucepan over medium-low heat, combine the cream, vanilla bean and seeds, and salt. Heat until small bubbles form at the pan sides, about 5 minutes. Remove from the heat and let steep for 10 minutes. Strain through a fine-mesh sieve into a liquid measuring cup. Discard the vanilla bean.

In a bowl, whisk together the egg yolks and the ½ cup sugar until light in color and texture. Slowly whisk in the cream.

Have ready 4 widemouthed half-pint jars with lids. Divide the custard evenly among the jars and let sit for 5 minutes. Then, using a small spoon, skim the foam from the surface of each jar. Screw on the lids until secure but not tight.

When the water reaches 176°F, using tongs, grip each jar and gently submerge them in the water bath. Cover the water basin with plastic wrap and cook for 1½ hours.

When the custards are ready, carefully lift the jars from the water bath and pat dry. Transfer the jars to the refrigerator until the custards are set and well chilled, at least 1 hour or for up to 1 day.

Remove the jars from the refrigerator at least 30 minutes before caramelizing the tops. Sprinkle each custard with about 2 teaspoons sugar and, using a culinary torch, melt the sugar until bubbly and lightly browned. Let the custards sit for 5 minutes to allow the topping to crisp, then serve.

2 cups heavy cream

1 vanilla bean, split lengthwise and seeds removed

½ teaspoon kosher salt

5 egg yolks

½ cup sugar, plus about 8 teaspoons for topping

Water Temperature: 176°F
Time: 1½ hours
Sealing Method: half-pint jars

SERVES 4

Poached Pears with Mascarpone Whip

You can use red or green D'Anjou pears here, or if you can find neither one, Bosc or French butter pears are two other good options. For a simpler topping, serve the pears with crème fraîche or plain Greek yogurt.

Prepare an immersion circulator for use according to the manufacturer's instructions. Preheat the water to 175°F.

Place the pear halves, wine, sugar, vanilla bean, lemon zest and juice, and cinnamon stick in a large locktop plastic freezer bag, arranging the pear halves in a single layer, and seal using the water immersion method (see page 10).

When the water reaches 175°F, lower the bag into the water bath and clip the top of the bag to the side of the water basin. Cook until the pears are tender, 1–1½ hours, depending on ripeness.

Remove the bag from the water bath, transfer the pear halves to a plate, and keep warm. Remove and discard the vanilla bean and cinnamon stick from the poaching liquid, then transfer the poaching liquid to a small saucepan. Bring the liquid to a boil over high heat, reduce the heat to medium, and simmer until the liquid is reduced to a thick syrup, about 10 minutes.

Just before the syrup is ready, make the whip. In a bowl, using an electric mixer or a whisk, combine the cream, sugar, and mascarpone and whip until stiff peaks form, about 4 minutes.

Place 2 pear halves in each individual bowl, coat them with the reduced syrup, and top with the whip. Serve right away.

Water Temperature: 175°F
Time: 1–1½ hours
Sealing Method: water immersion

SERVES 4

4 D'Anjou pears, peeled, halved, and cored

3 cups dry red wine

¾ cup sugar

1 vanilla bean, split lengthwise

Grated zest and juice of 1 lemon

1 cinnamon stick

FOR THE WHIP

½ cup heavy cream

¼ cup sugar

1 cup (8 oz) mascarpone

Chai-Spiced Apple Pie

Choose a good baking apple for this richly spiced pie filling. Gala, Northern Spy, Rome Beauty, and Golden Delicious are all good choices.

Prepare an immersion circulator for use according to the manufacturer's instructions. Preheat the water to 160°F.

In a large bowl, mix the brown sugar, cornstarch, cinnamon, salt, nutmeg, cloves, cardamom, and ginger. Add the apples and lemon zest and juice and toss to coat evenly. Place the apple mixture and its juices in a large vacuum bag, arranging the slices in a single layer, and vacuum seal closed.

When the water reaches 160°F, lower the bag into the water bath and clip the top to the basin side. Cook for 1–2 hours.

When the apples are ready, remove the bag from the water bath. Transfer the contents to a large saucepan. Cook over medium heat, stirring often, until the juices thicken, about 10 minutes. Spread the apples on a baking sheet. Let cool.

Preheat the oven to 425°F. On a lightly floured work surface, roll out a dough disk to a 12-inch round and transfer to a 9-inch pie dish. Add the apple filling. Roll out the remaining dough. Place on top of the pie. Trim the dough overhang, then pinch to flute the edge. Cut 3–5 small vents on top. Brush with the egg white, then sprinkle with the turbinado sugar.

Transfer the pie to a baking sheet. Bake until the crust is light golden brown, about 25 minutes. If the edges begin to burn, cover them with aluminum foil. Reduce the oven temperature to 375°F and continue baking until the crust is a deep golden brown, about 20 minutes. Transfer to a wire rack.

In a bowl, whip the cream to soft peaks. Stir in the maple syrup. Serve the pie with the cream alongside.

1 cup plus 2 tablespoons firmly packed light brown sugar

2 tablespoons cornstarch

2½ teaspoons ground cinnamon

½ teaspoon kosher salt

½ teaspoon ground nutmeg

½ teaspoon ground cloves

½ teaspoon ground cardamom

¼ teaspoon ground ginger

5 lb apples, peeled, halved, cored, and cut into ½-inch-thick slices

Grated zest and juice of 1 lemon

Pie dough for two-crust 9-inch pie (2 disks)

1 egg white, lightly beaten

1 tablespoon turbinado sugar

1 cup heavy cream

2 tablespoons maple syrup

Water Temperature: 160°F
Time: 1–2 hours
Sealing Method: vacuum seal

SERVES 10

Apple slices remain
firm and retain their
shape and texture
when parcooked with
sous vide precision.

To make the best shavings, warm a thick bar of dark chocolate between your palms or briefly in a microwave, then draw a vegetable peeler lengthwise along the bar.

Mexican Chocolate Ice Cream

Anyone who has ever sipped a cup of traditional cinnamony Mexican hot chocolate will recognize its influence on this dark, velvety chocolate ice cream. The creamy custard base cooks without curdling in low, slow sous vide heat.

Prepare an immersion circulator for use according to the manufacturer's instructions. Preheat the water to 185°F.

In a blender, combine the chocolate, vanilla seeds, milk, cream, sugar, cocoa powder, egg yolks, cinnamon, cayenne, and salt and process on high speed until thoroughly mixed and smooth, about 2 minutes. Pour the custard into a locktop plastic freezer bag and seal using the water immersion method (see page 10).

When the water reaches 185°F, lower the bag into the water bath and clip the top of the bag to the side of the water basin. Cook for 45 minutes–1½ hours. When the custard is ready, remove the bag from the water bath. You can either immerse the bag in a large ice-water bath until well chilled or refrigerate the custard in the bag overnight.

Transfer the contents of the bag to an ice cream maker and freeze according to the manufacturer's instructions. Serve the ice cream right away, or transfer to an airtight container and place in the freezer for up to 1 month.

To serve, spoon into individual bowls and garnish with the shaved chocolate.

Water Temperature: 185°F
Time: 45 minutes–1½ hours
Sealing Method: water immersion

MAKES 1 QUART

7 ounces dark chocolate, roughly chopped, or chocolate chips

1 vanilla bean, split lengthwise and seeds removed

2 cups whole milk

1 cup heavy cream

½ cup sugar

¼ cup Dutch-processed cocoa powder

6 egg yolks

1 teaspoon ground cinnamon

¼ teaspoon cayenne pepper

¼ teaspoon kosher salt

Shaved dark chocolate, for garnish

BASIC RECIPES

FRITES

¾ cup water

½ teaspoon sugar

½ teaspoon baking soda

1–1½ lb russet potatoes, peeled and cut lengthwise into batons ½ inch by ½ inch thick

Canola oil, for deep-frying

Prepare an immersion circulator for use according to the manufacturer's instructions. Preheat the water to 194°F.

In a liquid measuring cup, whisk together the water, salt, sugar, and baking soda to make a brine. Place the potatoes in vacuum bag and pour in the brine. Arrange the potatoes in a single layer and vacuum seal closed.

When the water reaches 194°F, lower the bag into the water bath and clip the top of the bag to the side of the water basin. Cook the potatoes for 15 minutes. When the potatoes are ready, remove the bag from the water bath. Drain the potatoes, discarding brine. Spread in a single layer on a paper towel–lined baking sheet and let dry for 20 minutes.

Fill a large, heavy-bottomed saucepan three-fourths full with oil and heat to 225°F on a deep-frying thermometer. Line a baking sheet with paper towels. Working in batches and using a slotted spoon, lower the potatoes into the hot oil and fry until golden, about 5 minutes. Transfer the potatoes to the prepared pan. Repeat until all are fried.

Increase the oil temperature to 380°F. Line a second baking sheet with paper towels. Again in batches, lower the potatoes into the hot oil and fry until golden brown, about 2 minutes. Transfer to the prepared pan and season with salt. Repeat until all the potatoes are fried. Serve hot.

Water Temperature: 194°F
Time: 15 minutes
Sealing Method: vacuum seal

SERVES 2–4

PARMESAN POLENTA

4 cups chicken or vegetable broth

1 cup yellow cornmeal

Kosher salt and freshly ground pepper

1½ cups grated Parmesan cheese

¼ cup crème fraîche

2 tablespoons heavy cream

4 tablespoons unsalted butter

In a saucepan over high heat, bring the broth to a boil. Slowly whisk in the cornmeal. Reduce the heat to medium-low and cook uncovered, whisking occasionally, until the cornmeal has absorbed the liquid and is tender, about 10 minutes. Season to taste with salt and pepper. Continue to cook, whisking, until thickened, about 3 minutes. Remove from the heat. Whisk in the Parmesan, crème fraîche, cream, and butter. Keep warm until ready to serve.

SERVES 4

HERBED MASHED POTATOES

2 lb Yukon gold potatoes, peeled
and thinly sliced

½ cup heavy cream

4 tablespoons unsalted butter

2 cloves garlic, smashed

Kosher salt and freshly ground pepper

3 tablespoons minced fresh chives

2 tablespoons minced fresh flat-leaf parsley

1 tablespoon minced fresh basil

1 teaspoon minced fresh thyme

Prepare an immersion circulator for use according to the manufacturer's instructions. Preheat the water to 194°F.

Place the potatoes, cream, butter, garlic, and 2 teaspoons salt in a roughly even layer in a large locktop plastic freezer bag and seal using the water immersion method (see page 10).

When the water reaches 194°F, lower the bag into the water bath and clip the top of the bag to the side of the water basin. Cook for 1½ hours.

When the potatoes are ready, remove the bag from the water bath and transfer the contents to a large bowl. Using a handheld masher or a food mill, mash the potatoes. Stir in the chives, parsley, basil, and thyme and season to taste with salt and pepper.

Serve right away, or let cool, cover, and refrigerate, then gently rewarm in a saucepan over medium-low heat before serving.

Potato–Celery Root Mash

Substitute 1 lb celery root, peeled and thinly sliced, for 1 lb of the potatoes. Cook with the potatoes as directed. Omit the herbs.

Water Temperature: 194°F
Time: 1½ hours
Sealing Method: water immersion

SERVES 4

MAPLE-GLAZED CARROTS

1 lb carrots, peeled and cut crosswise
on the diagonal into ½-inch pieces

2 tablespoons unsalted butter

2 tablespoons maple syrup

1 teaspoon kosher salt

Freshly ground pepper

2 tablespoons chopped fresh flat-leaf parsley

Prepare an immersion circulator for use according to the manufacturer's instructions. Preheat the water to 194°F.

Divide the carrots, butter, maple syrup, and salt evenly between 2 locktop plastic freezer bags and add a few grinds of pepper to each bag. Seal the bags using the water immersion method (page 10).

When the water reaches 194°F, lower the bags into the water bath and clip the top of each bag to the side of the water basin. Cook for 30 minutes.

When the carrots are ready, remove the bags from the water bath. Heat a large frying pan over high heat. When the pan is hot, empty the contents of the bags into the pan and cook, stirring constantly, until the liquid reduces to a glaze, about 3 minutes. Stir in the chopped parsley and season to taste with salt and pepper. Serve hot.

Water Temperature: 194°F
Time: 30 minutes
Sealing Method: water immersion

SERVES 4

MEXICAN CORN ON THE COB

4 ears corn, shucked

4 tablespoons unsalted butter

10 fresh cilantro sprigs

1 jalapeño chile, halved lengthwise

Kosher salt and freshly ground pepper

½ cup minced red onion

½ cup chopped fresh cilantro

½ cup crumbled Cotija cheese

½ cup sour cream

1 teaspoon grated lime zest

1 teaspoon fresh lime juice

Pinch of ancho chile powder

Prepare an immersion circulator for use according to the manufacturer's instructions. Preheat the water to 183°F.

Divide the corn evenly between 2 vacuum bags. Add 2 tablespoons butter, 5 cilantro sprigs, ½ jalapeño chile, and ½ teaspoon salt to each bag. Arrange the corn in a single layer and vacuum seal closed.

When the water reaches 183°F, lower the bags into the water and cook for 30 minutes.

While the corn cooks, in a small bowl, mix the onion, cilantro, and cheese. In another small bowl, stir together the sour cream and lime zest and juice and season to taste with salt and pepper.

When the corn is ready, remove the bags from the water and transfer the corn to a plate. Heat a stove-top grill pan over high heat. Add the corn and cook, turning often, until evenly charred, about 5 minutes.

To serve, arrange the corn on a platter, drizzle with the lime sour cream, and top generously with the cheese mixture. Sprinkle with the ancho chile powder and serve right away.

Water Temperature: 183°F
Time: 30 minutes
Sealing Method: vacuum seal

SERVES 4

TOMATO-CUCUMBER SALAD

2 cups cherry tomatoes, halved

2 cucumbers, peeled and shaved lengthwise into ribbons

1 red onion, very thinly sliced

4 tablespoons extra-virgin olive oil

1 tablespoon sherry vinegar

3 tablespoons fresh oregano leaves

Kosher salt and freshly ground pepper

in a bowl, combine all the ingredients and toss gently to mix well. Cover and refrigerate for at least 20 minutes or up to 1 hour before serving.

SERVES 4

POACHED EGGS

6 eggs

Prepare an immersion circulator for use according to the manufacturer's instructions. Preheat the water to 145°F.

When the water reaches 145°F, using a slotted spoon, carefully lower the eggs into the water bath and cook for 45 minutes.

When the eggs are ready, remove them from the water bath with the spoon. To serve, gently crack each egg into a small bowl, then slide the egg from the bowl directly onto each dish.

Temperature: 145°F
Time: 45 minutes
Sealing Method: water immersion

MAKES 6

INDEX

The Sous Vide Cookbook

Conceived and produced by Weldon Owen, Inc.
in collaboration with Williams Sonoma, Inc.
3250 Van Ness Avenue, San Francisco, CA 94109

A WELDON OWEN PRODUCTION
1150 Brickyard Cove Road
Richmond, CA 94801
www.weldonowen.com

WELDON OWEN, INC.
President & Publisher Roger Shaw
SVP, Sales & Marketing Amy Kaneko
Finance & Operations Director Thomas Morgan

Associate Publisher Amy Marr
Senior Editor Lisa Atwood

Creative Director Kelly Booth
Art Director Marisa Kwek
Production Designer Howie Severson

Printed in China
First printed in 2017
10 9 8 7 6 5 4

Associate Production Director Michelle Duggan
Imaging Manager Don Hill

Library of Congress Cataloging-in-Publication
data is available.

ISBN: 978-1-68188-398-4

Photographer John Lee
Food Stylist Kim Kissling
Prop Stylist Kerrie Sherrell Walsh

Weldon Owen is a division of Bonnier Publishing USA

ACKNOWLEDGMENTS

Weldon Owen wishes to thank the following people for their generous support in
producing this book: Lexi Hager, Shelley Handler, Stephen Lam, Josephine Hsu, Becca Martin,
Carolyn Miller, Elizabeth Parson, Sharon Silva, and Genesis Vallejo.

AMANDA HAAS is the Director of Culinary for Williams Sonoma and oversees the test kitchen. She is also a cookbook author and founder of the website One Family One Meal. She is a graduate of Tante Marie's Cooking School.

EMILY MCFARREN is a cook in the Williams Sonoma Test Kitchen. She has worked in the kitchens of several San Francisco restaurants, including Frances and Marla Bakery, as well as in event planning and food styling. She is a graduate of the San Francisco Cooking School.

ISABELLE ENGLISH is a cook in the Williams Sonoma Test Kitchen. She has also worked as a food stylist and photographer and is the founder of The Belle Jar, a bicoastal catering and event company. She is a graduate of New York University's Gallatin School, where she concentrated in food studies and visual art.

INKEN CHRISMAN is a cook in the Williams Sonoma Test Kitchen. She has expertise in food writing and recipe testing and development. She is a graduate of the University of Virginia and Tante Marie's Cooking School.

JOHN LEE is an award-winning photographer based in San Francisco. He works primarily as a food and portrait photographer, but his roots are in photojournalism. He has photographed more than a dozen cookbooks, including Tyler Florence's *Fresh* and Williams Sonoma's *Luscious Fruit Desserts*. John approaches food photography from a gastronomic and cultural anthropologic perspective.